A Visit to THAILAND

by Charis Mather

Minneapolis, Minnesota

Credits

All images are courtesy of Shutterstock.com, unless otherwise specified. With thanks to Getty Images, Thinkstock Photo, and iStockphoto.

Cover – Wutthichai, Day2505. 2 – SOUTHERNTraveler. 4-5 – Zen S Prarom, creativestockexchange. 6-7 – grebeshkovmaxim, TWStock. 8-9 – Take Photo, Sean Pavone. 10-11 – Sean Pavone, Pikoso.kz. 12-13 – vectorx2263, Vassamon Anansukkasem. 14-15 – AnnelieNuxoll, Tatiana Tverdunova. 16-17 – Avigator Fortuner, puwanai. 18-19 – naito29, prasit jamkajornkiat. 20-21 – topten22photo. 22-23 – sittitap, NUTCHANAT SANSUT.

Library of Congress Cataloging-in-Publication Data is available at www.loc.gov or upon request from the publisher.

ISBN: 979-8-88509-378-1 (hardcover)
ISBN: 979-8-88509-500-6 (paperback)
ISBN: 979-8-88509-615-7 (ebook)

© 2023 Booklife Publishing
This edition is published by arrangement with Booklife Publishing.

North American adaptations © 2023 Bearport Publishing Company. All rights reserved. No part of this publication may be reproduced in whole or in part, stored in any retrieval system, or transmitted in any form or by any means, electronic, mechanical, photocopying, recording, or otherwise, without written permission from the publisher.

For more information, write to Bearport Publishing, 5357 Penn Avenue South, Minneapolis, MN 55419.

CONTENTS

Country to Country 4
Today's Trip Is to Thailand! 6
Chiang Mai 8
Temples 10
Khon Dance 12
Khao Sok National Park 14
Floating Market 16
Food 18
Lopburi Monkey Festival 20
Before You Go 22
Glossary 24
Index 24

COUNTRY TO COUNTRY

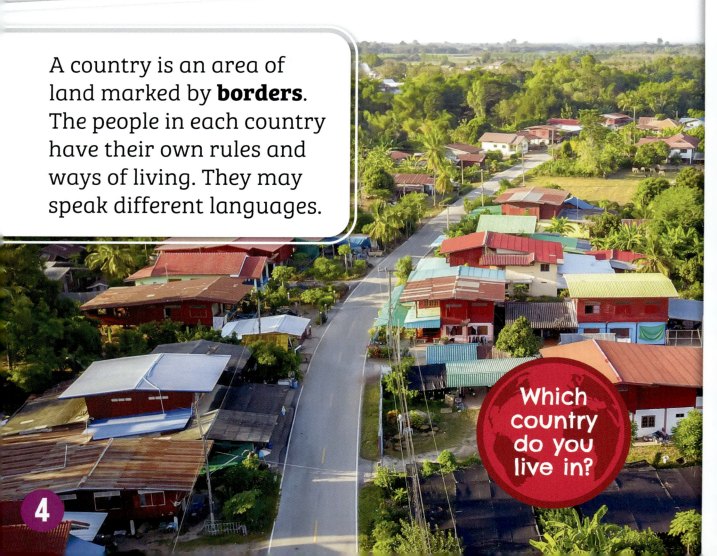

A country is an area of land marked by **borders**. The people in each country have their own rules and ways of living. They may speak different languages.

Which country do you live in?

Each country around the world has its own interesting things to see and do. Let's take a trip to visit a country and learn more!

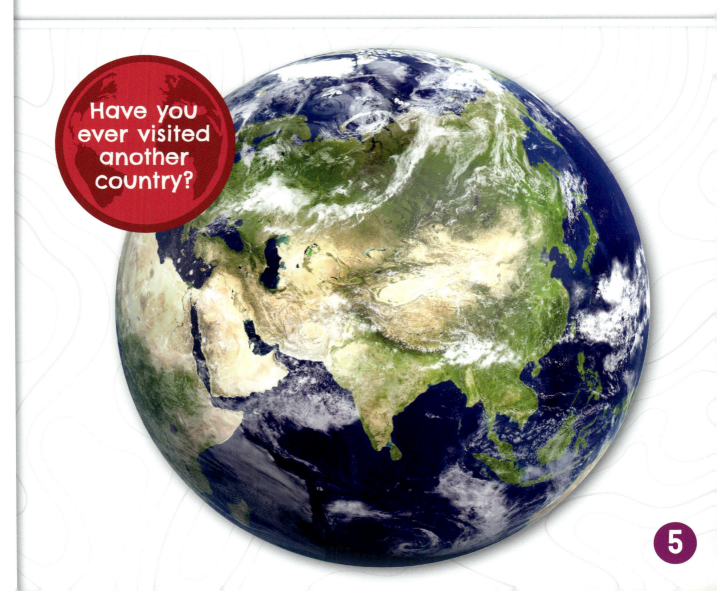

Have you ever visited another country?

TODAY'S TRIP IS TO THAILAND!

Thailand is a country in the **continent** of Asia.

FACT FILE

Capital city: Bangkok
Main language: Thai
Currency: Baht
Flag:

Currency is the type of money that is used in a country.

CHIANG MAI

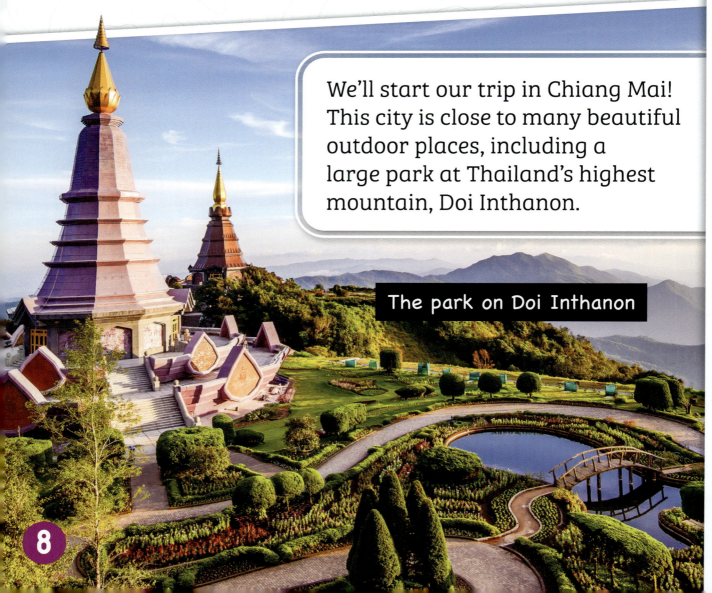

We'll start our trip in Chiang Mai! This city is close to many beautiful outdoor places, including a large park at Thailand's highest mountain, Doi Inthanon.

The park on Doi Inthanon

The Old City's moat and walls are shaped like a square.

To learn about Chiang Mai's history, we can visit an area called the Old City. It is separated from newer parts of the city by walls and a **moat**.

TEMPLES

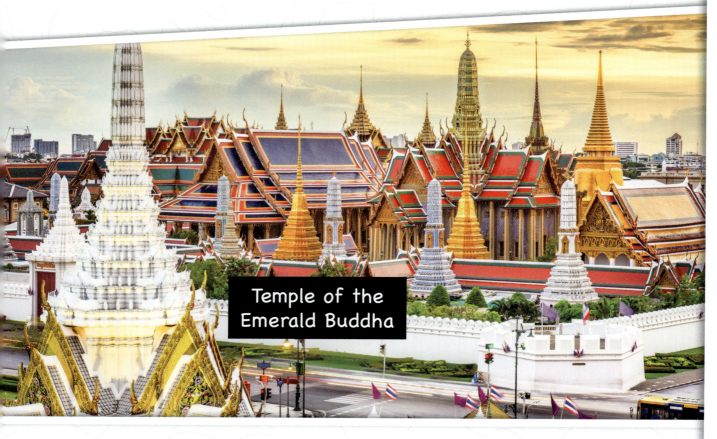

Temple of the Emerald Buddha

Temples are an important part of Thailand's history. The country has thousands of them. Many of the temples are large and colorful, including the Temple of the Emerald Buddha.

One modern temple called Wat Rong Khun is unusual because it is almost completely white. The temple is covered with tiny, detailed decorations.

Wat Rong Khun

KHON DANCE

Next, we'll go watch some dancing. *Khon* is a **traditional** Thai dance that tells a story. *Khon* dancers dress up in masks and **costumes**. They dance to special music.

The story told by the dancers has hundreds of characters. Thai children learn about it in school. Some even learn to perform the *Khon* dance.

Khao Sok National Park

Let's head into nature! Khao Sok National Park is covered by a rain forest. It is home to many different kinds of plants and animals, including wild elephants.

Khao Sok also has a lake with amazing, towering rocks that are covered with trees.

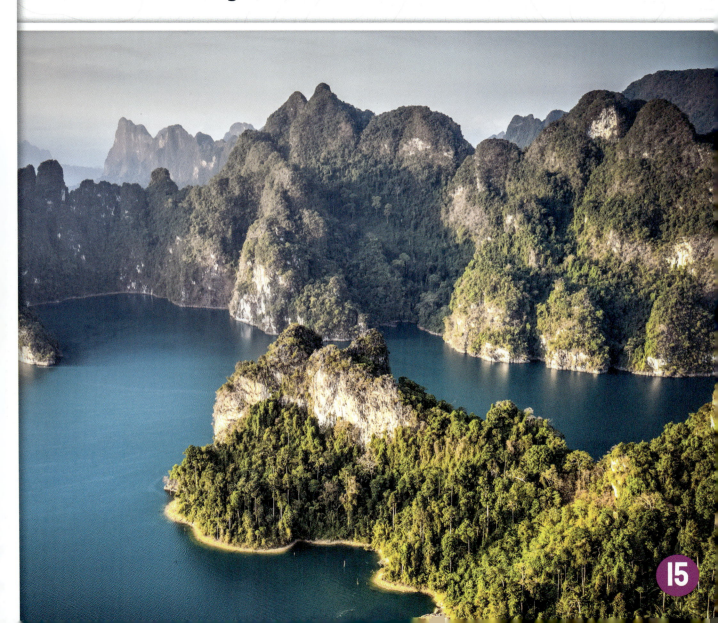

FLOATING MARKET

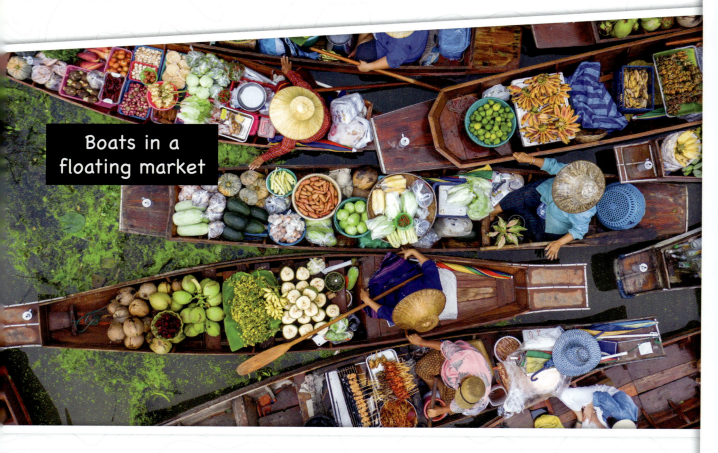

Boats in a floating market

Feeling hungry? We can grab a snack at a floating market in the city of Bangkok. These markets are in **canals**. People ride boats slowly down the canals and sell things.

Many boats have fruit and other food. Customers can shop by riding in their own boats. They can also stand at the edge of a canal and stop sellers' boats as they float by.

FOOD

One of Thailand's most well-known foods is called *tom yum*. This spicy soup is made with shrimp, lime juice, and lemongrass.

For dessert, let's try some mango sticky rice. This sweet dish is made of rice mixed with coconut milk and served with sliced mango.

Lopburi Monkey Festival

Time to celebrate! The town of Lopburi has a **festival** every year to celebrate the thousands of macaque monkeys that live there.

During the festival, people put out huge piles of food for the monkeys. The animals eat as much fruit as they want while people watch from nearby.

Feeding the monkeys is thought to bring people good luck.

BEFORE YOU GO

We can't forget to visit Phraya Nakhon Cave. During the day, sunlight shines through an opening in the roof of the cave. It lights up a small building that was made for a king many years ago.

We could also visit Thung Salaeng Luang National Park. It is a great place to go on walks and enjoy nature.

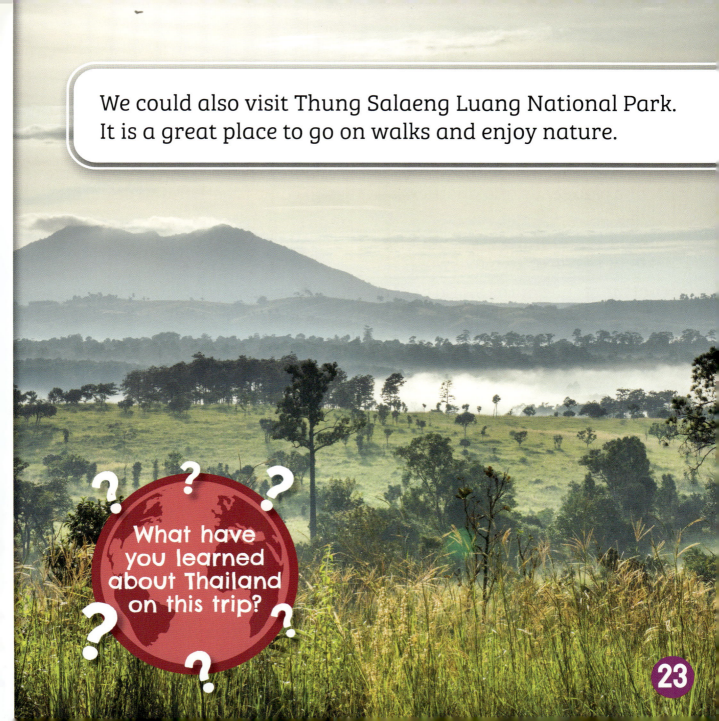

What have you learned about Thailand on this trip?

GLOSSARY

borders lines that show where one place ends and another begins

canals small waterways built for boat travel or to move water

continent one of the world's seven large land masses

costumes clothes worn for a special reason

festival an event for lots of people to come together and celebrate

moat an area of water around a building or town used to keep it safe from attacks

temples buildings where people go to pray or worship

traditional relating to something that a group of people has done for many years

INDEX

boats 16–17
canals 16–17
dancing 12–13
food 17–19, 21
monkeys 20–21
mountains 8
parks 8, 14–15, 23
rain forests 14
temples 10–11